THE ABCS OF LOVE

CHITRA NAIR

Made with ❤ on the Notion Press Platform
www.notionpress.com

This is for all those souls out there, who have experienced love in some way or the other.

Contents

Contents

Preface

I am not a jilted lover.

At least, I think I'm not.

But I'm a very emotional person, though. And a pretentious know-it-all-who-in-all-honesty-doesn't-know-it-all.

And that's why, here I am, writing about love, which should ideally be written by jilted lovers.

But then again, if Seema Taparia, with her 100% fail rate, could have an entire Netflix reality show on matchmaking, then why can't I write pretentious poetry about *love*?

(No offense to Seema Aunty, in all seriousness, though. We should actually thank her for making the first lockdown in India much more bearable with *Indian Matchmaking*. Really, I mean it. Or maybe not. xD)

So here it is.

The ABCs of Love. Written by a girl who, in all honesty, has a very… *distorted* perception of it.

Enjoy reading!

Or give this book to a library.

Or *raddi*, if you want to make money, *jhatpat fatafat*

Acknowledgements

I don't think writing this would've been possible without seeing and experiencing love in so many vibrant forms.

So for my family and best friends, who made me believe in the power of love, *thank you.*

Falling

If I must confide,
Love is like a roller coaster ride,
Be it romantic or not,
The highest of highs you're bound to sought;
And then before you know it,
You descend into a chaos that none can stall,
Until you hit the lowest of lows as you fall;

1. A Long Time Ago

A long time ago,
When fairy tales were real,
You, like many other fools,
Believed in the magic of love;
You thought you were a damsel in distress,
Waiting for a knight in shining armour;
You thought you were the lost princess,
And your Prince Charming, right around the corner;
Yet here you are now,
Still wondering, still waiting,
For the myth,
Called Prince Charming;
There are some around you,
Who say, your dream guy's worth the wait,
Stay patient, stay calm,
Even if it may look a tad bit too late;
And there are some,
Who actively deride you,
For not settling for any Tom-Dick-Harry with money,
For them, let's be honest, you're mid, honey;
You may never know, darling,
Your epic Romeo may just be around the corner,

Or what if, he's the one,
Trapped in the pages of your history,
Bound to make an appearance,
Some time in the near future;

Note:

There's hope for everyone: someday, somewhere, sometime
Keep believing, keep thriving.
If it feels too much, mute all the couples on your Instagram who post way too much PDA. It's much more peaceful then.

2. Boy, oh boy, I wish you were mine

They say,
Everyone keeps a checklist, you see,
Of all the things they want,
In their true love-to-be;
And here I am,
A Type A type to a T,
With a PhD thesis,
On how the love of my life is to be;
But the truth is?
God up there has quite the funny bone,
Loves to shake things up,
And set a completely different tone;
Before I know it,
I fall, head over heels, you see,
For someone who's far apart,
From my dream-husband-to-be;
You, for sure, look the part -
Tall, fair and,
So goddamn handsome,
And oh boy, you're so damn fit!

Yet you, my love, are a puzzle,
That not even Einstein can decode,
How on earth they made you,
Is what only God can encode;
Yet, no matter how much I deny,
I'm drawn to you, like a moth to a flame,
I don't know why,
I don't know who to blame –
I don't think all the words are enough to,
Express how you are so unapologetically you,
With a mind-boggling swagger,
You see that blind confidence in only a select few.
Boy, oh boy,
I wish you were mine,
Oh, if life were like a romantic comedy,
You'd be by my side always – wouldn't that be so divine?

Note:
This is for all the girls out there, who've had crushes that they've no control over.
For me? It's a love letter to a guy from my college who looked like a desi Edward Cullen.

3. Charm in Chaos

In a utopia,
There would be no souls,
Wallowing in their own toxicity,
Unleashing wrath with their megalomania;
In a utopia,
There would be no broken hearts,
Who can't wait to start,
Wreaking some havoc of their own;
But the sad truth is,
We live in a world,
That's a far cry,
From this idyllic paradise;
And here you are,
Deep diving into a tornado,
Of angst-ridden torment,
Completely unaware,
Of the destruction,
That you're about to encounter;
For like many lost warriors before you,
You find charm in chaos,
You find beauty in agony;
But before you know it,

You're cascading down,
An abyss of endless pain and loss;

4. Dark Spaces

Sometimes in life, during some phases,
You fall for those,
Within whom you see,
The dark spaces,
That plague,
Your tormented soul;
They are so woefully wrong,
Yet so irresistibly right,
You try your best to ignore them,
Yet they're never once out of your sight;
You know they are not the chosen ones,
Yet, in some way,
It feels like they're
The perfect fit for you,
The parts that make you whole,
The ones that mirror,
The dark spaces,
In your aching soul;

Note:

This is the result of watching Gehrayiaan's trailer a little too many times.
I had some unrealistically high expectations from that movie and the poem? Turned out to be not quite the same.
But I like it.

5. Eight Letters, Three Words

Words may not look it,
But they hold power,
Way more than you can imagine,
Or see it fit;
You know what?
There are some words longer than sentences,
That have a Rabelsalat of letters,
But mean diddlysquat;
And then, there's 'I love you',
Eight letters, three words,
Doesn't look that scary,
But it's the most overpowering of them all;
Some say, saying 'I love you',
Is a sign of weakness,
A key to allow access,
To be mocked, to be walked all over on,
Yet, the ones who do say it,
Are a lot braver than that,
To be able to embrace that,
Someone means a lot to them;

The ones who do say it,
With all sincerity, heart and soul,
Are the ones who truly, deeply care;

6. Fatal

For most in fairy tales,
Love is simple -
Boy meets girl,
Girl meets boy,
They fall in love,
Happily ever after,
The end.
But reality hits a little harder,
Love is a lot more fatal,
Boy meets girl,
Girl meets boy,
Girl falls hard,
Boy doesn't care enough,
Unhappily ever after,
The end.

7. Gone Before Goodbyes

Many moons ago,
There we are,
At the cusp of the world's newest disaster,
Feels like it's come sooner, much faster –
And there I am,
On the phone with you,
Talking about all things sundry,
And not even realizing truly –
That it would be the last time,
I'd hear your voice;
That it would be the last time,
That you'd be around;

A few days later,
I get to know that you're gone,
Left us behind,
Without even saying goodbye;
All of a sudden,
With no notice,
I feel like everything has stood still,
Nothing will ever be the same, never will;

All of a sudden,
All the old memories keep rushing,
Like a tornado,
And I'm left torn apart, thinking –
You were gone before saying goodbye;
And the worst part is?
I don't even remember,
My last words to you;
As I drown in my thoughts,
I grasp at the straws,
Reliving, reimagining,
What did we talk about, at last?
I think I remember something,
But deep within,
I know that that's not it;
That's not how our last conversation went;
Who would've thought, really?
That it would be the last time,
I'd hear your voice;
Oh, believe me, if I had the choice,
I'd have never said goodbye;

Note:
This is for one of my dearest members in my family, who passed away right around the time the pandemic hit. It was sudden, and heartbreaking.

I miss her, every day.

8. Her and Him

Her

I was told that there are five stages of grief,
With each stage, you grow, there's a sense of relief;
But when your heart's broken beyond repair,
You find yourself in that same vicious cycle, again and again;
Every day I lie to myself,
Tell myself that you're a thing of the past,
That we were never ever meant to last;
But then -
I run into you, at a cafe, one fine day,
Out of the blue, in every way;
I see you with her, incandescently happy,
In a way that you were never with me;
Before I know it,
Waves of grief rush over me again,
Reminding me, like a cackling never-well-wisher,
Of my never-ending pain -
That I was never good enough,
Not today, not tomorrow, never;
I take a deep breath,
To stop myself from crying,
And tell myself, yet again,

That I'm still alive, not dying -
In the depths of your misery;
And then, I pick up my book again,
Telling myself an affirmation,
That I'm getting over you - some day;

Him

I was told that, you can never feel bad,
If you broke someone's heart if you never cared enough;
I know I'm supposed to be glad,
I'm with someone easy, someone less convoluted;
Yet every day, I lie to myself,
Tell myself that you're a thing of the past,
That we were never ever meant to last;
But then -
I see you at a cafe, seated by the window, one fine day,
Out of the blue, in every way;
I see you reading your favourite old book,
It amazes me how much at peace you look -
Than all the times,
You and I were together;
Before I know it,
Waves of guilt rush over me again,
Reminding me, like a cackling never-well-wisher,
Of my never-ending pain -
That I was never good enough for you,

Not today, not tomorrow, never;
I regret the way I treated you,
Every single day, always;
And tell myself, yet again,
I'd rather be with her than,
Inflict you with pain beyond measure;
You, my love, are a treasure,
I wish I could tell you
how much you meant to me,
But ah well,
Now's not the time anymore, you see;

9. In the cobwebs

One day, you wake up,
Thinking that everything's new,
A fresh slate, a fresh start,
But deep within your heart –
You know that,
Your shrouded in the cobwebs,
Of a past that never seems to go away,
A ghost of familial love, that still stays;
They tell you, that it's over, it's long gone,
It's a chapter in your life's history,
But it's a chapter your keep replaying,
Cause historycan repeat itself, no?
But in this case, will that be?
Or should you accept facts for facts and let it go, be free?

10. je ne sais quoi

Some have beauty so easy to trace,
Some have an abundance of grace,
Some have treasures beyond measure,
Then there are some, who have all three at once;
And here you are,
Feeling forlorn,
Doubting yourself, all day,
Every step of the way;
You wonder why,
You're never noticed,
Neither by your blood, nor by your friends,
When will this era of being overlooked end?
Yet, you may not know it,
But you too have,
Je ne sais quoi -
That's what makes you rare;
You may not know it,
But you have something in you,
That lies in a few,
And it's about time -
You discover that;
Some may love, some may not,

But it is nothing for you to be so distraught;
You have to, at first, accept yourself;
For you may not know it,
You have, within you,
Je nais sais quoi,
That's what makes you you,
Never ever change that,
Not today, not ever, come what may;

Note:
There are so many times when we doubt ourselves and don't think that we're worthy of love.
But we are. For we have within us, something that is so unique, something so rare. And more than anything else, we need to learn to love that and ourselves as whole, no matter what.

11. Kaleidoscope

A sepia tinge,
Faded edges,
Leaves you,
With an aching twinge;
You think,
Pictures say a thousand words,
But the truth is, they,
Lead you to the brink –
Of a rollercoaster down,
The memory lane,
A kaleidoscope of blurred moments;
You go down a dive, that for sure,
Makes you drown,
In a simpler universe,
Where everything was easy,
Conversations flowed deep,
Certainly not terse;
But you know?
It's truly a shame,
That photographs won't let you,
Go back to that era, ever again;

12. Language of Grief

Grief is such a funny place to be,
It feels like you're never ever free,
From being sad, angry, empty – all at once;
And the worst bit?
If you're not the grieving party, pray,
What on earth can you even say?
Can you assure them in your pretentious glory?
Or stay in stunted, stone-cold silence?
The language of grief,
Is that there's nothing you can truly say,
Or do that can bring back the ones lost,
No matter what the cost;

Note:

The pandemic era truly made me realize how... difficult it is to be in grief all the time. And how helpless you feel when you're surrounded by those who have gone through a crippling loss.
What can you say? What can you do?
You have no idea, indeed.

13. Mirage

A sea of canoodling couples -
Some in love with the idea of one another,
Others together, shrouded by the shadows of,
What will people say?
And there you are,
Far apart,
Wondering what it's like,
To be actually in love;
Is it just butterflies fluttering,
Bashful stares, coy stuttering;
Or is it what they show in the movies,
Heightened passion in the best of fashion,
Completed with dramatic pauses, followed by rounds of applauses?
Yet whatever it is,
For you, it is now a mirage,
And you finally feeling grateful,
For your warm entourage;

Rising

They always say you *fall* in love,
You're a fool, you're doomed, yada yada yada;
But you know what the real love is?
The one where you *rise* in love -
You do better, you be better,
And know that the ones you've chosen to love,
Are by your side, so,
As to help you grow;

14. No Love Lost

I remember a time,
Where there were a few,
I deeply, truly adored,
And one of them was you;
I was a silly little girl,
Searching for an idol,
And there you were -
Pretty, introverted and rib-ticklingly funny!
I remember boasting,
About your greatness;
I remember toasting,
Your success;
I was a little peacock,
Only not as wondrous looking;
And you were the rain,
Giving me pure, unadulterated joy!
But days passed,
Faster than a ray of light;
Seasons changed,
And unfortunately, so did you;
You became more beautiful,
You became more confident,

You became more popular,
You became someone I didn't know;
The last few times I saw you,
You weren't the sweetheart that you used to be;
You weren't the person I used to worship, day and night;
You turned out to be as real as a charlatan!
A phony smile plastered on your face,
A proud attitude you had put on,
A false person you had become;
Oh darling, you became a perfectly plastic Barbie doll;
I hated the way you walk,
As if you were better than the rest;
I hated the way you talk,
As if you know a great deal more than the geniuses;
I didn't know who you were,
I didn't know what you wanted;
I didn't know why were you,
Alienating me like this!
Did you not remember,
That little girl with whom you used to play?
Did you not remember,
Making that little girl's day?
I don't know how to express this even now,
But I did miss the old you
The shy person that you used to be,
Only an extrovert in front of me;
Years have passed, see,

And I did hope against hope,
That we may go back to where we used to be,
But I guess, that's not meant to be;
I feel all right now,
For I've grown, and so have you,
I don't hold that resentment anymore,
For what transpired;
I know now it wasn't meant to last,
The sisterhood between you and I;
Here I am now, and I say this with a sigh:
We grew up to be too different,
And went through too many diverging paths and journeys,
Ultimately, that bond between us? T'was never meant to be;

<u>Note</u>:
This as a revised version of the poem I wrote, nearly 9 years ago. It's based on a true story, for an older sister, who's a stranger now. She was someone I looked up to, she was someone fun.
I don't feel bad anymore, just have a twinge of pain, while I think about how hollow our bond's become. I've grown up, she's grown up - it was bound to happen.
But those emotions in this poem? They were real. And I'm sure people would've experienced that, some time in their lives.

15. Old-School Romance

In the golden era of,
Hook-ups, break-ups and dating apps,
An old-school romance, perhaps,
Is a rare sight to see;
It's no longer all about,
Stealing stealthy glances,
Taking forbidden chances,
Or weaving the greatest saga of love;
Now, it's all about,
Merrier strings of lovers the more,
Settling old scorned scores –
V for Vendetta indeed;
Why, I truly bemuse,
Is it so tough to see,
An old-school romance free,
From superficial stereotypes of today?
Is it because,
We've lost the will,
To find love that'll fulfil,
Our innermost happiness?
Is it because,
We've lost the desire,

To find someone who truly sets our heart on fire;
What is it, really?
In the golden era of,
Hook-ups, break-ups and dating apps,
An old-school romance, perhaps,
Will never be seen, ever again;

16. Peggy in the World of Joans and Bettys

First, there are the Bettys,
A la Audrey and Grace Kelly,
The ultimate epitome,
Of old-world sophistication;
Then we have the Joans,
Who the Marilyns ape,
Beautiful, brilliant,
Yet oh-so-fierce;
The Bettys and Joans of this world,
Are great women with great strengths,
Are the ones the world takes note of,
Wherever they go, whenever they go;
And finally, we have the Peggys,
Driven, dedicated, hard workers to the core,
Never a part of the age-old,
Romantic lore;
The Peggys of the world,
Climb up the ladders of the jungles,
Fumbling, tumbling, stumbling,
Ultimately, they get where they want to be;

Yet, they find themselves,
Unlucky in the matters of the heart -
Right from the start,
Where they meet an assortment of losers plenty;
While they thrive,
In their professional lives,
They deeply pine,
To have true love by their side;
Finally, as the Peggys grow,
And find the North star in their career,
They find in themselves,
A sense of confidence;
Then, one fine day, before they know it,
They find love in their dearest of friends,
That keeps them,
Happy and healed, always;

Note:

This poem is inspired by my admiration for the three fabulous queens of Mad Men: Joan, Peggy, and Betty.

They are all, in their own ways, amazing. But the difference is?

The Bettys and the Joans know it and own it.

The Peggys of the world? They really need to work hard to get there. And often, they need someone to encourage them to do so.

17. Questions

Generally, I am the one,
Who is extremely clear,
And can discern, without fear,
Who's hers and who's not;
Yet you've proved to be a puzzle,
You've managed to bamboozle,
With your razor-sharp words,
And your befuddling allegience;
When I think of you,
I'm often left with,
Deep, soul-searching questions few,
That cannot be answered easily;
Why do you glorify some,
And make them feel oh-so-mighty?
Why do you have icy words,
Or stone cold ignorance to bite me?
But isn't it strange?
When you dramatically fall,
It's not your royal clout,
But rather the dowdy old me you call?
Yet, when you've risen again,
You set me aside,

And flock around with your so-called loved ones,
Somehow, this makes me ask -
Can I even call you a loved one?
Can I tell you about my anxieties and fears,
When you don't treat me like a normal person,
Much less a dear?
Why is it,
When you speak to me,
Not in times of normalcy,
Only when you deam it fit?
Why is it,
That in front of the world,
It's only me,
You constantly reprimand?
These questions, while they continue to plague me,
I think I'd rather be wise, see,
To let go of the possibility,
That you'll treat me normally;
In that, I find peace,
Than wallow, yet again, in the ruminating torment;

Note:

Have you ever wondered why some people don't like you?
They could be your frenemies or some members of your family - who just behave in the oddest way that's cruelly cutting?
This poem is for those people.

18. Rebecca, Oh Rebecca

Humans are said to be flawed to the core,
So goes the age-old lore –
Yet, there are some like you, see,
A perfect amalgamation of Athena and Aphrodite;
Rebecca, oh Rebecca,
Beauty, brains – you had it all;
In my life's tale, you were the star,
And I, a nameless stranger;
Wherever I went, wherever I saw,
You were the deal, the main draw;
People sang your praises to the sky,
I couldn't ever match up, even if I were ever to try;
Rebecca, oh Rebecca,
Wealth, grace – you had it all;
In my life's tale, you were all the light,
And I, shrouded in the darkness of night;
Yet, I had some respite –
The man I loved, told me about your embittered spite,
Turns out, you're not the perfect angel after all,
No matter how high you rose, the higher was your fall;
Rebecca, oh Rebecca,
You name a thing – you had it all,

Yet when you had the world at your feet,
How could you care be so casually cruel?
He said you were truly the nightmare of nightmares,
With torture as your second nature, followed by a string of affairs;
And how you goaded him, as you saw fit,
Into a sin that he had but no other choice to commit;
Rebecca, oh Rebecca,
Back when I was a young girl,
I was haunted, horrified by your ghost -
Ever so ethereal, ever so surreal, ever so real;
But now, as I'm older,
I truly, deeply wonder,
Were you really in the wrong?
Or were you penalized so for not getting along,
With the notion of how the society,
Saw women of those times to be;
Rebecca, oh Rebecca,
Beauty, brains – you had it all;
In my life's tale, you are now the victim who put up a good fight,
And I, just a helpless sympathizer of your sorrowful plight;

Note:

A long time ago, my mother came across this book by Daphne du Maurier.

And I remember her recommending it to me, all earnestly.

Since I felt lazy at the time, I read the Wikipedia summary. And since then, the story's stayed with me.
This poem is for all the Rebeccas out there, who at the outset, are the personification of perfection. The ones who are both admired and abhorred, in equal portions. And yet, are the ones who need to be seen in a new light, so that we can, for once, somehow sympathize with their plight.

19. Sweater Weather Lover

Looks like it's that time of the year,
When everything's cosy, everyone's kind;
And there you are, right 'round the corner,
Lingering in the back of my mind;
I wonder if I should,
Fall back into the same old patterns of before,
Send you a text, give you a call,
Repeat, yet again, the same old lore –
My mama tells me not to do it,
She doesn't see it fit,
For me to drown in the pools,
Of your spiraling tornado of toxicity;
My friends roll their eyes at me,
They, more than anyone else, can see,
How you were up to no good,
Not then, not now, and not ever;
Yet here I am, whiling my time away,
Wondering if I should,
Go back to my sweater weather lover,
I mean, I actually could –

But would you still want me back?
Or would you like it if I stayed away,
Watched you from afar as your life goes astray?
What do you want, really?

Note:

I listened to 'Tis the damn season' a little too many times and I wrote this. This poem is totally inspired by that.

It's really about contemplating what-ifs, you know? The narrator of this poem won't go back to that toxic person. Rather, she is just mulling over the possibilities.

20. Tata Breadcrumbs

I remember you,
Not very well,
(Thank God for that),
But you're the one,
Who always had,
An interesting story to tell;
I remember you,
Waltzing into my friend's life,
Like a chaotic hurricane,
Sweeping her off her feet,
And then leaving her all alone,
In endless strife;
And here you are again,
Sliding in, like nobody's business,
Yearning for her attention,
Not because you care about her,
But because, you love to see her,
Crumble at your words like a crying mess;
Why do you think,
Strewing breadcrumbs of love will,
Help you get her back?
Why do you think,

My best friend isn't a human being,
But a toy for you still?
Who the hell do you think you are,
Thinking that you can have her back,
When honestly, you certified jackass,
It's not her, it's you,
With your hot-and-cold schtick,
*Are one among the many f*ckbois who lack –*
The privilege of being truly loved;

Note:
To all the exes of my best friends, this is for you.
Apply some aloe vera to the burn. Hope it helps.
Your toxic presence in my best friends' lives doesn't. So there's that.

21. Unconditional

They say there are two types of loved ones -
The ones that take,
All that's there in their wake;
And the ones who give endlessly;
The givers are the ones that matter,
They bring you the joy of endless laughter;
Even in your sorrows, they're around,
No matter what they're always there;
They love you for who you are,
Not for your laurels,
They are there for you,
Whether you're near or far;
Their love for you is unconditional,
No constraints, no baggage,
No pain, no red-hot rage;
No matter what happens,
You know, for you, they'll alwas be there;

22. War of Hearts

In a world full of moony-eyed loons,
Besotted in love,
There's an unsung majority of broken lovers,
Who won't discover happiness anytime soon;
Some drown in their own misery,
Wallow in endless pools of pain,
Some stay strong,
For they see there's not much to gain –
In pining for the ones that got away,
The ones who never meant to stay;
And then we have the legion,
Of those wronged souls,
Scorned deeply into becoming,
Embittered ghouls;
The heartbroken soon,
Become the heartbreakers;
Who now, in their frenzied vengeful glory,
Seem to have gotten a lot of takers;
It's vicious, the war of hearts,
Some don't go down without a fight -
That unleashes havoc,
Destroys everyone, destroys themselves;

Yet the ones who win the war,
Are not the heartbreakers plenty,
Rather are the ones who find this carnage meanignless, empty,
And embrace the warmth of peace and letting go of this nonsense;

23. xoxo // Yours Truly

Instagram, these days,
Is a wedding album on steroids;
You see strangers become soulmates,
In a matter of 10 dates;
And subtly, your folks,
Are buckling under the weight of insidious pressure,
Kind of like Atlas underneath the sky;
You overhear your nosy relatives and nosier neighbours pry;
"How about your girl?
Are you going to keep her aside,
Like a rotting bread,
Why not find a Suitable Boy instead?
To all those interested,
In the Sahara Desert that's your love life,
Here's what you should say,
So that they (finally) go away:
I'd rather find love that has meaning,
Over something so superficial, so ephemeral;
You may think it's cool to be soulmates in 10 dates,
But it's my life, I'm not playing house,
Let me be as I am,
Don't you tell me what to do or grouse;

I'd love to say the four-letter word that starts from F,
But I'm assuming you're not getting any of that IRL,
So that's why your nose fell,
Into my business,
Anyway, adios,
Take care, never come by again, leave me be;
XOXO,
Yours truly;

<u>Note:</u>
I cheated.
But there's hardly any word that starts from X! Unless you want me to make a poetry about a Xylophone or a Xerox machine.

24. Zen

You're a fool,
If you think life is a linear path;
It is in, all honesty,
An endless pool –
Of waves, tornados and more,
Sweeping you away,
From the path,
You thought was in store –
For you in the end,
Yet, in those hurricanes,
You find your peace,
You're on to mend –
The bleeding wounds,
That never seem to go away;
You're on the path to heal,
You'll see, you'll get there soon;
You may not have found,
The one who set yet your heart on fire,
But you discovered a stronger soul,
Buried deep underground –
Within your own mountains,
Of insecurity and pain,

You found your zen,
In that spirit, who you see when –
You look in the mirror,
Completely at ease,
With themselves,
Accepting the fact that –
Life isn't a linear path,
But whatever it is,
It's a wonderful start,
To an unforgettable experience;

Thank You.

For taking your time out to read this. Poetry is not easy. And me spamming you endlessly sure wouldn't have been easy.

But anyway.

Love is such a complicated emotion, you know? I don't know if it was even possible to cover so many facets of it, when I've not experienced it fully myself.

Some of the poems, like 'A Long Time Ago', 'je ne sais quoi', and 'Zen', are my attempt to encourage the reader to love themselves. Accept themselves for who they are - flaws and all. And they are different stages, you know - pre, during and post-heartbreak seasons.

Then there are some, like 'Dark Spaces', 'Peggy in the World of Joans and Bettys', and 'Rebecca, Oh Rebecca', which are completely taken from my love for pop culture. Something, which has also defined my perception of love.

And finally, there are poems like 'Her and Him', 'Questions', and 'No Love Lost', which are adapts of the poems I've written in the past regarding love. And writing them? Was cathartic and liberating. Especially to understand how my emotions have evolved since then.

I am making it categorically clear, though: some of the familial poems are based on true stories. None of these poems have any resemblance to my real life love stories.

Why? Because I'm still single.

Yet, here I am, writing about love.

If Sima Aunty can talk about it, I can sure as heck write about it.

Take care.

XOXO

Chitra

P.S. Any typos, grammatical errors in my poems are to be construed as poetic license and will be rectified once I'm informed of them.

Printed by Libri Plureos GmbH in Hamburg, Germany